In A Dark Room...

With Highlights of Maroon

A Collection of Poems

Sheree N. Johnson

ISBN: 0-9974182-0-6
ISBN-13: 978-0-9974182-0-0

ACKNOWLEDGEMENTS

~ For all the couples that go back like babies and pacifier

CONTENTS

AND IT BEGINS...

… Rows of crumbling tombstones
Drawn here like flies to paper
Learning about past lives
Upon lies
And still I rise

Stay thirsty with me my friends
And you'll become Wise
Like chips
Internationally known
I'm a Grooown Woman!
Now betcha I run this…

Maroon is *love*...
It's *blood*...
It's *pleasure*...
It's *pain*...
It's **me**...

The Past Life and Times of *Sheree*

~Fruits of Passion

Escapade

A boxed room about 8ft. in height and 7ft. in width

Dark as the moonlight sky

A white light peeks through the window

To caress the pearl white tub in multiple places

And kiss the pearly white toilet

Teasing the concrete colored carpet-like covering

Two silhouettes

One standing tall and the other on the sturdy white sink

Two bodies creating motions like waves in an ocean

Shadow Blinds

In a small dance studio

Late at night

He closes up shop and cuts off the light

Only to hear music from the connecting door

He cracks open the blinds…

Guess what he saw

A divine being that flows like the sea

Like liquid fire, she dances beautifully

Her body sways with every rhythmic beat

He's stuck and amazed

Can't move HIS feet

Caressed by the darkness that engulfs the room

Her body is kissed by highlights of maroon

The rich color glows outside the window pane

The setting enhanced

By sounds of summer rain

Entrapped by her movement

As her inner light shines

She lives in that moment

And dances between the lines…

Love Is...

Love is a sensation

Caused by temptation

When a man puts his dictation

Into a woman's combination

Do you get my conversation or do you need a demonstration?

He may say he loves you and you'll say it too

But when your stomach starts rising

He'll ask what the hell's wrong with you

    60 minutes of pleasure

    9 months of pain

    3 days in the hospital and a baby without a name

The father's a bastard

The mother's young no more

This wouldn't have happened

If the rubber hadn't tore

The Secret

Honey, you know what you feel - -
It's not the real deal

Keep it on the hush hush

With your hands on my thighs
And lush in your eyes
You say…

Keep it on the hush hush

I say
Your woman is upstairs
You say
Who the hell cares?

Keep it on the hush hush

Sneaking out at night
What a sight

Keep it on the hush hush

You keep buying me things
Still wearing your wedding ring

Keep it on the hush hush

You won't leave me alone
I take your secret home
And if you can't fuel your crush, lush
You keep dialing my phone
I play like I'm not home

I'm about to give your life strife
I'm talkin' to your wife

When you're not at home

You're about to get bum rushed

That's right... I had a secret
But I'll be DAMNED if I

Keep it on the hush hush

Lovesick

To be in love with you is freedom in a cage,

Blind sightseeing a performance on stage

Enamor has no bounds

It's rounds of a lifetime combined with forever

Clever kites made of wings

Birds that sing silhouettes so softly and clear

You can hear them from the highest mountain top

Stop to free your mind from the issues of today

Clear a path with a breeze

A straight-away through the clouds,

And past the sun

We can only experience adoration

When our mind, body and soul are one

I'm sorry...

I'm love-sick

Ice Cream Stand #1

Ice cream

Ice cream

Ummmmmmm….

How I love my ice cream

Vanilla ice cream covered with a thick layer of chocolate fudge

Ummmmmmm…

It's like sludge in my mouth

With its smooth creamy flavor

My mind goes South

I think back and rewind

To a time to a time that I can only describe as divine ecstasy

I lick the tip

And crunch munch on the nuts

I lick the tip

And crunch munch on the nuts

Oh how I love to put the chocolate fudge in my mouth

And suck all my favorite vanilla flavor out

Embrace the cone and swirl my tongue

No more vanilla meant I was done

So back to the original question at Stand #1

"Cup or cone?"

A cone of course!

Because they're so much more fun

Mind~Fu*k

Mandingo, Mandingo

Look at the size of your shaft

Mandingo, Mandingo

Let me work my craft

I want to lick... your stick

To... swirl my tongue

I want you to feel my erotic sensations

On your hard

Thick

Johnson

Promise to please `till you cum inside this heavenly split

Feel the warm juices

The liquids in my mouth

Enchanted Apple gets ready

Pumpin' punany fluid out

Tell me you'll fuck me `till I hit a high note

I'll put your cucumber down my throat

`Till I damn near choke...

`Till I damn near choke...

`Till I damn near choke on your

Long strong Donkey-Kong Mandingo dick

I... won't lie

I... don't lie

I give good head

Hard yet?

I want you to embrace my butter-soft smooth skin

Warm is the temple of sin

And generous are the juices within

I'm ready to begin the session with him

It… He… Sugar daddy…. Boo

As you lay the pipe in the perfectly pulsating purity of my punany

Stroking in and out

Of my tight… wet… juicy pussy

Ssssshhhhh

Secret~Fu*k

I want to verbally penetrate your membrane

Through insane perversions of sexual seduction

I'll

Light your fire and inspire lyrical illusions

Causing our words to entwine

From the fusion of our minds

You see

I'd like to share brain cells with you all the time

I can stimulate your shaft

And tantalize your testes

By caressing verbs so vigorously there's no need to embellish

By kissing similes so sensuously it makes metaphors jealous

Uuuhhh

Mind~Fu*k

Shopping

One day after shopping, I met this girl named Victoria on **Saks Fifth Avenue**.

She was mad cute with a little **Baby Phat**, thick too.

So I stepped to her and asked, "Can I get a minute to **Converse** with you?"

No doubt I had to **Express** to her what I was feeling inside.

"I **Guess**," she replied.

That's when I took her by the hand, looked her deep in the eyes and called her my **Bebe.**

One hour later we back at my place, giving each other hickeys,

She says, "I'm getting hot" and starts coming out of her **Dickies**.

I grabbed a condom and adjusted my **Lenscrafter** so I could get a **Sharper Image** of her **Apple Bottom.**

Ready to go, armed and strapped,

I whispered in her ear, "Can I put my **Banana Republic** inside your **GAP**?"

She said, "Boy I'm feeling you, but there is no need to rush;

Besides, I'm a freak. So you know how we do, those **Toys R' Us.**"

I told her, "Let's skip the foreplay and throw on your favorite song,

So I can take you to the **Bed, Bath & Beyond**."

She agreed, so I proceeded with haste;

placed her on top of my **South Pole** while making **The North Face**.

"It's so **Diesel**! She gleefully screamed.

So loud an **Ecko** could be heard throughout the apartment, or so it seemed.

A minute later, after everything was said and done,

She turned to me and said, "I'm only 17, though I'm mistaken

Forever21."

Now that's something that I can't condone,

So I told her, "Please leave my **Gracious Home**."

I never did see her again and that's how I would like to keep it.

What took place that day, well... will forever remain me and **Victoria's Secret**.

Eye

Eye spit sounds of music...
The melody
that is Corey
courses through my mind
Entwined with notes that makes my body wine
Like it's being coached by Aphrodite
You C...
4 me
Music
Is
Love
Eye will love you like kids love cake
I wanna love you so close
your scent pours
out my pores
when I sweat
I wanna get down like the Swedish
And make love to you like a tempurpedic
Our bodies fit the mold
as we hold one-another
and intimately explore each other's holes
under the covers
The kind of love that makes Stevie
wonder
A love for the ages
Eye want a world where you become my escape
A world where you're the only option I want to take
I wanna be high school sweethearts
just so we can have more time together
Tell people how we weathered all storms
as delicious light forms around us
At just
The right
Time
Eye wanna love that knows how to unwind
Kick back so we can relax our minds

And
Enjoy a "conversational piece"
I want that… aaahhhhh…
Take that how you wanna
Eye wanna love you so deep
That your soul becomes enlightened
as the reflex zones on your sole
tells me what your body likes
And
Eye wanna love that makes the Earth quake
like Quaker Oats boiling in a pot
          without a top
Exploding over everything you got
I want you to be mu
Last
First
Kiss
I never wanna miss you
How I miss you
when I kiss you
before I leave for a trip
Slip into a lust-filled trance
As I dance around the room
in your curve-scented Fruit of the Loom shirt
I wanna love you until it hurts
May I love you?
You C
4 me
Music
Is
Love
The melody
that is Corey
courses through my mind
I spit sounds of music
From time to time…

S&M

I will always remain
a
positive experience within the membrane.
This is a verbal penetration for your mind.
I assigned my pussy a name –
     Enchanted Apple
Not red delicious apple
No
Not granny smith apple or golden apple
No
Enchanted Apple
"If this town is just an apple, then let me take a bite…"
Mike was right
I'm sure he was delighted to
sample the sacred place of a woman that
makes you slip into a punany dream.
Example…
Come here daddy…
Let me lick… your jimmy
until it's slick with my spit
so you can slide into this heavenly split.
Causing waves of sweet juices to flow down my core
     From the G-spot you hit.
If I bend over doggy style,
could you keep up with it?
Habla me…
Like an orchestra
Can you stroke my chords like a perfectly tuned cello?
Can you move me like the fingers of a classical pianist?
Can you breathe love into me through your instrument?
Caress my soul with your presence
Untold stories of future moments
past
I envision your lungs pregnant with oxygen
     that brings about your joyous laugh
Thought of you run through my mind

like a firecracker string of warmth and pure delight
Your bow is right when it comes to caressing my violin…
See
we can make heavenly music
Let us begin…
Around you, my heart rate rises
Away from you I turn pale
But with you in me,
I can…
Scale the highest mountain top like Sophia Danenberg
Raise my sail like Doris Miller
Tell tall tales like Hans Christian Anderson
Long stories
Short pauses
And nothing but sweat, estrogen and testosterone in between.
I mean…
Hair pullin', ass grabbin', pelvic thrustin' exstacy.
"Yes I want to be loved,
Oh GOD I want to be loved.
But now I want a quickie.
No bit marks, no scratches
No hickies.
If you can get with that
Then papi come get with me."
You see
It's not the length
It's not the size
It's how many times I can make it rise
Make you feel like you're home
When you're in between these thighs
I'm waiting…
Anticipating…
Your
verbal penetration for MY mind.
I will always remain
a
positive experience within the membrane

Visualize my pleasure…
Feel my *pain*…

~Historical Urbanization

Released

Whipped `cause I was first begotten

Falling on the golden ground

Realizing that my life is rotten

Hearing words without a sound

Realizing that my life is rotten

Seeing my blood flow in a stream

Trying to make my problems forgotten

By seeping into a daydream

Trying to make my problems forgotten

A'last I die before I wake

The ground – My body did not rot in

My soul is cleansed for the lord to take

Steal-a-way

Steal-a-way, steal-a-way, steal-a-way,

The heart blows into a rapid beat.

Running on your feet all day,

Yet getting caught up in defeat.

Taken back to the plantation lands,

Being dragged and pulled through grime.

The overseer hangs him by his hands

And whips him `till the end of time.

Steal-a-way back to the beginning,

The beginning is also the end.

Is the water

Is the soul

Is the source

Is the paradise he has always dreamed of.

Torture of the First Child's Slave

Whipped `cause I was first-begotten

My hands were tied together securely

The rope on my feet had to follow

The blood from my body exploded like a volcano without a sound

My people won't be forgotten

The whip bites off pieces of flesh slowly but surely

My body feels so hollow

But my soul will not be found

By the souls that bound me, I was begotten

I was whipped ever-so harshly

My people felt such sorrow

As I feel straight to the ground

Black Is...

Black is the color of my ancestors;

Black is the way I was born,

Black is the stereotyped as pure evil;

Black is our image being torn.

Black is the cat that gives you bad luck;

Black is that hole in your socket,

Black is the color of the sky at night;

Black is that book in your pocket.

Black is killings between cultures;

Black is the gun that you hold,

Black is the beauty of my land;

Black is the Earth growing old.

Black is responsibility bravely chanted;

Black is the cross of sweat of a nations' rise,

Black is the boy who knows his heroes;

Back is the way a hero dies.

Blind Cooperation

My people are led by **a temptation**

caused by all legislation

and **administration.**

They think minorities are like wild animals

but that's not my realization.

Minorities are like oxymorons

depending upon their given situation.

It's Mary Jane that **spreads** over young minds like butter

and causes **a world-wide sensation**

to the point **where** we all need immunization.

Red

Black

Yellow

Blue

Cats and dogs have the best sensation of seeing

Colors would be all in our imagination

if we would just stop the participation

of dehumanization.

Generation X **is becoming** the alienation of **civilization's** creation.

We have to realize we've been freed by the **Proclamation of**

Emancipation.

Since all of this is given information

it should need no elaboration or citation.

Nor should it need an explanation.

We need to **put down the guns and drugs and pick up a logical conversation**.

Some minorities would rather have street recreation

than have a true school education.

We may seem like endangered species in school

Because we don't want to go through the 4 year duration.

Can we start a demonstration

proving our determination

of having no more manipulations

amongst our congregation?

Marching and smiling

showing our manifestations of joy

because we are no longer at a limitation.

The Voices I Hear

I walk a path directed by free will,

escorted by an ancient unheard choir;

The voices of the dead are with me.

The voices of the dead are with me still,

response – I think – an intense desire;

I walk a path directed by free will.

But hearts and minds are made, for good or ill,

and all that came before our genes acquire.

The voices of the dead are with me still.

The old man's walk, his weakness instilled;

with all your strength – try to quench his fire.

I walk a path directed by free will.

Alone now, I have drank and had my fill

my sacrifice, my life, will inspire;

The voices of the dead are with me still.

I can't find all that my heart desires

without the song of that ancient choir.

I walk a path directed by free will;

The voices of the dead are with me still.

Chanting for Knowledge

Those songs were our only way of saying

What we were too scared to actually say

Those songs were our only understanding

Of what we could not comprehend

Why were we brought here?

Why were we brought here to these oppressive plantation lands?

How did we end up being the ones?

Why were we chosen for this bitter joke from the lord of fates?

Through the songs

We described slavery as it was

And made fun of the Masters

We raise the wheat,

They give us the corn;

We bake the bread,

They give us the crust;

We sift the meal,

They give us the skin;

And that's the way they take us in.

We skim the pot,

They give us the liquor,

And they say that's good enough for the nigger.

The big bee flies high,

The little bee makes the honey.

The black folks make the cotton,

And the whites get all the money.

Deceased Wife

Weep not, weep not

She is not dead;

She's resting in the bosom of God

Heart-broken am I – weep no more

Grief-stricken son – weep no more

She's only just gone home

Immigration

Force

Slavery, hurt

Beating, crying, traveling

Unhappy, laws, freedom, enjoyment

Exciting, dancing, working

Fun, benefits

Choice

Red nails
Running through chest *hair*
Like a *fire*
Through a *forest*

~Poetry Shorts

Meow

Sleek and sexy

Fine and divine

Always landing on their feet

Cats are beautifully made feminine

Rough Garden

I look at the leaves upon the ground.

Either yellow or gold,

Growing,

Growing,

And then rots down.

Beautiful

Her soft laugh was sunshine and rainbows

Entwined in delicious light

That will last forever

Busy Café Gossip

The waves of hot coffee were lost

Like empty city café echoes

We sunk beneath the door

The shop smoked conversation

My Name

Sheree

He

Her

She

See

Her-She bars

Keep things spicy and interesting...

Tu' cuerpo

Yo quiero tu' alma para

    volar como un pato en el cielo.

Yo quiero tus manos para

    nadar como pez en el rio.

Yo quiero tuslabios para

    Cantar como un pajaro en la pradera.

Beautiful

Her soft laugh was sunshine and rainbows

Entwined in delicious light

That will last forever

Ode to Spam

Encased in a metal coffin – preserved

With myriad artificial chemicals.

The pinkish flesh is saved and later served

In small, convenient, bite-sized particles.

But, oh! The price at which this meal is bought!

A thousand screaming piglets trapped inside - -

Suspended, gleaming, in an oily clot

Just waiting, waiting to be eaten fried.

The dark blue coffin,

Locked

with metal key,

Can only hide the violence for so long,

And when it's opened, frightened eyes shall see

The slaughtered thousands in their greasy throng.

   O meat! Thou thing, thou aspirant to ham!

   With horror paralyzed we name the SPAM!

Words lingering in the air like cigarette smoke…
Heavy…

~Reality Check

Lyrical Illusions

I have my pen

Which has its blue ink

But what to write

I cannot think

My brain is that gun shooting knowledge like boom

My poetry book holds these verbal holes

So they don't disappear into deadly fumes

Let me take your mind away from all its cloudy days

Have you acting crazy and running wild in several different ways

At the same time

I'm

That lyrical tornado that spirals through every school

That up-to-date computer virus that hackers think is cool

That new-age Encyclopedia for your CD-ROM

Telling you stories about Vietnam

Who invented .com

And all about bahm... bahm... bahm... The Obamas

Let my poetic vapors get you high off of thought

A chain reaction for my pockets

Show them my book you just bought

And tell your friends not to be hurt if they can't catch my vapor

Some people can't grasp the concept of black thought

On white colored paper

Take off your mind's jacket

Get comfy in your bed or chair

Let your thoughts soar without despair

Reach over to get some paper and a pen with lots of ink

So you can write down everything you thought of

And now think

Leap of Faith

On top of the building ledge

Seeing bright lights and action.

Wondering why I was put on Earth.

Wondering why people are here at all.

Feeling the cold air rush into and through my skin.

Pushing and pulling me

Back and forth

From left to right

Hearing the sounds of traffic, I stand clear-headed.

With bright lights still gleaming everywhere, I take

The Leap of Faith

Falling down fast, seeing the lights come closer and closer

Hearing traffic coming more nearer toward me

I made a mistake

A single tear drops from my left eye

Now all I see is darkness

No gleaming bright lights

No sounds of traffic

No more me

But a tear

Eurhythmy

I'm the lyrical illusion

Of brain contusions when I rhyme

Confusion engulfs the mind

And you become blinded by the words

Divine verbs and nouns

Profound adjectives and compounds

Put together at the perfect time

I rhyme

Line after line my imaginative flow

Glows like liquid fire

As I aspire to reach new heights

As a poet

With new levels of greatness

I take this gift

And sift through the trials and tribulations of my life

Reflect on memories that haven't caused me strife

On my knees I pray for life, love and true bliss

Use my words as a catalyst

I'm floetic like Floetry

It's poetic because it's me

Hear the spoken words that were meant to be free

My words fly like bullets

And my knowledge spreads like vapor

Once I put my verbal piece

On any color paper

My broken promise

My life is a broken promise

A mistake in life am I

Half my life has been pain and sorrow

And yet I don't know why

I cry almost every night

Nobody sees my pain

I'm a young woman with many troubles

I'm starting to love the rain

Why does life periodically seem bad?

Why was I even born?

Where's my place in this world?

I struggle for my image not to be torn

I'm going nowhere fast

And going somewhere slow

I like to dress up, cook, clean and bake

But only a few people know

High school wasn't always easy

Sometimes I just wanted to leave

But certain family expected me to do so

So I stayed,

Just to succeed

I'm an aged woman in a young woman's body

My life is already sung

Been though depression, pain and heartache

Always singing… I will overcome

My life is a broken promise

A mistake in life am I

Half my life has been pain and sorrow

And yet I don't know why

I cry almost every night

Nobody sees my pain

I'm a young woman with many troubles

I'm starting to love the rain

Date of Emergency

September 11th, also known as 911,

Is the date of emergency that weighs a ton

On our heads and our hearts

Since it was the art

Of terrorism that brought down our financial district.

Yet I still ask, "Was it really worth it?" and "Why did they risk it?"

Flying into what Nostradamus called the twin brothers in the New City.

All those human lives gone to waste... what a pity.

The first thing I thought of when I saw the two planes crash,

Was the oh so famous question Marvin Gaye asked:

"What's goin' on? Oohh what's goin' on?

Mother, mother

There's too many of you crying.

Brother, brother, brother,

There's far too many of you dying."

Everyone came together all around our nation,

And made a powerful demonstration,

Showing a family standing tall.

We are ALL brothers and sisters in the long run.

It's not fun to see GOD's children perish.

I cherish the memory of the nation's candle light vigil;

It will be remembered in history books.

Yet it looks as if the next generation might be damaged

By a wound so deep, no bandage could heal.

The healing mechanism has a psychological appeal.

See, on the television screen,

It looked like human toy figurines.

Or even paper,

> But that's not so.

The children who were there really know.

They saw bodies leaping from 80 stories high

Out of windows in the sky;

> Even the bald eagle had to cry.

Witnessing the World Trade Center peeling like a banana

Caused me to worry about family, friends, and a...

A new question that I came across...

Will we be forced to have a World War III or IV?

What is to become of our peaceful skies?

What will happen to the safe, soft lullabies?

Will we start sleeping to the cries of bomb threats?

The high-pitched bomb siren is something one never forgets.

I'm in question.

Do you want to know my suggestion?

Peace be with you...

Live long and prosper...

FUCK IT!!!

Build a memorial,

Take that fucking tutorial off my colored box,

Get back to reality so stocks can rise,

Whoever catches that "terrorist"

> Give him a prize!

Forgive, just don't forget,

And let's move on with our lives.

2 wrongs don't make a right...

Let our darkness be our guiding light.

The Ocean In Me

I am an ocean,

So calm, yet so forceful

I am an ocean,

So soothing, yet so harsh

I am an ocean,

So shallow, yet so deep

I am an ocean,

So different and unique

I am an ocean,

So untamed, so mystique

I am the ocean

That rides up on your shores

I am the thing so natural

And filled with such riches and beauty

The ocean so polluted

Yet so clean

The ocean so filled with waves

Of excitement and passion

I am the ocean,

I dare you to come and swim with me

Normal N.Y.C. Morning

It's 6am

Time to wake and start off my day

Don't want to get out of bed, but I have to

I have my daily morning stretch and my morning yawn

I look outside

See how the sky makes the city look gray and dull

It's raining

My house... my apartment

It's warm and comfortable while it's cold outside

Crows are flying around right now

Still tired

The rain makes me feel lazy

Want to go back to sleep

But I go take a shower and come back ¾ awake

I get dressed and make sure I smell like baby power

Leave the house....

My day has just begun

In a Dark Room ... With Highlights of Maroon

It is here I stand

In a dark room

Reprimanded by my past

I stand strong but still weak

Tweaking my inner consciousness

I seek to become the awakened one

It took me some time but I finally fixed my 20/20 blindness

You see

My past casts shadows of negativity over my life

I was suffering from spiritual withdrawal

I let the curves of my hips and thighs guide me

Like Sandra, I became Black Girl Lost

Looking for this woman I know as me

Sheree was hiding in her own skin

She lost herself within

"If you see Sheree, please tell her to come home"

I cried again and again

Watching my pain and suffering but I still didn't comprehend

As I abstained from my sexual vice

I gained knowledge without having to give brain

After all

Every pleasure contains within itself a small seed of pain

Most people produce plans but I didn't have any

I knew I had to weather the storms not forecasted

And there was gonna be plenty

I can't protect myself when I'm exposed

But the will of GOD will never take you

Where the grace of GOD will not protect you

Everyone knows

Black Girl lost was found with assistance

 I came to be one with myself...

No longer lost in the distance

Searching for a love to bring my flowers to full bloom

In My Dark Room...

With Highlights of Maroon

Reality

There's no such thing as reality to me

Life is like a play

My life anyway

Trying to please a convincing audience

To keep them going, to help me survive

Cause if there's no people and only lies,

There's no friends, only wonder whys

The audience is the people you talk to, smile at, and laugh with

The people who talk about you momentarily

But don't know you for the rest of your life

It's not a play that I wrote but it's one of a kind

Special just for me

No script, so I'm performing blind

It's extemporaneous, not thought of,

Off-hand and unpracticed

It's a deadly dream when you don't know

How long you're going to live

What will they label you tomorrow?

What you will be known for...

What you will do in life...

How do I proceed? How will I succeed?

Someone is watching me; every step that I take

When I turn a corner, who will be there?

Will I scream; will I laugh?

Will I be surprised; will I die?

Before I see the next day,

How many times will I cry?

There is no such thing as reality to me

Life is like a play

My life anyway

The Process

I need a pen and paper

    To clear my mind

I need the quietness and calmness

    Need to... find me some time

To relax my thoughts

    And put my body at ease4

My imagination starts flowing through my membrane

    As I feel a cool sea breeze

In New York City

 As I dwell in the Bronx

  And sit in my room

I bloom

Lyrically

 A melody

Oh say

 You can't see me

  On the beach

I teach

 Only those who wish to be taught

Feeling distraught

 I knew I had to reach deeper within my thoughts

Put down the pen and paper

    So words could be brought

    Into my mind

Again words hit the paper

At designated times

This is how I write my poems

And my rhymes

Train Thoughts

Waiting on the subway platform

Watching deaf friends sign so loudly

My stomach swells from gas

Like a sail impregnated by wind

I speak fluent metaphors

My skin holds traces of bricks and concrete

I'm from the Bronx

That's where my heart beats

Under my skin lives claustrophobic insecurities

My thoughts suffocating within

Leaving no choice but to seep through my pores

Scores of passengers ranking each other…

No cause

Mahogany complexion engulfs my body

True colors dripping like wet paint

My flesh is used to protect the mess within

Some days I want to hide under my skin

In the shade of my eyelids

Vulnerable blues create the hue

Eyes fall constant like summer rain

Even when I wanted to evict myself

And cried on a daily basis

To not be the basis of negativity

I refused to abandon this building

I daydream of a mind fuck of the highest notion

A brain orgasm from an exotic notion

People seeing me without preconceived notions

There are currently more sentences in prisons

Than there are sentences in which I could relish

I'm not trying to embellish

But I kiss similes so sensuously

It makes metaphors jealous

Here's my stop.

ABOUT THE AUTHOR

Whether she's launching public relations campaigns or putting her emotions to verse, Sheree N. Johnson remains committed to her love of language. Johnson is a seasoned account manager with more than ten years of experience at a Manhattan public relations firm. She drives teams to success through product launches, content production, strategic plans, and high-level events. When not immersed in work, she travels and focuses on the arts, including poetry, drawings, and dance. Her love of the arts drew her to slam at the Nuyorican Poetry Café in New York City. A graduate of Alfred University, Johnson earned a master's degree of professional studies and a bachelor of science degree in communication studies with a focus on public relations. She minored in English with a focus on writing.

Johnson, a Bronx native, continues to live in the borough. She is engaged to Corey L. Thomas.

www.ingramcontent.com/pod-product-compliance
Lightning Source LLC
Chambersburg PA
CBHW022342040426
42449CB00006B/682